The Teen Girl's Go

Social
survival

AM I
Cute
OR WHAT?

How to Have Fun and Feel Confident in More than 50 Situations!

By Jessica Blatt

Illustrated by Cynthia Frenette

Watson-Guptill Publications/New York

Senior Acquisitions Editor: Julie Mazur
Editor: Cathy Hennessy
Designer: Margo Mooney
Production Manager: Alyn Evans

Text copyright © 2007 by Jessica Blatt
Illustrations copyright © 2007 by Cynthia Frenette

First published in 2007 by Watson-Guptill Publications,
Nielsen Business Media, a division of The Nielsen Company
770 Broadway, New York, NY 10003
www.watsonguptill.com

ISBN-10: 0-8230-1726-5
ISBN-13: 978-0-8230-1726-3

Library of Congress Cataloging-in-Publication Data
Blatt, Jessica.
    The teen girl's gotta-have-it guide to social survival : how to have fun
and feel confident in any situation / by Jessica Blatt ; illustrated by
Cynthia Frenette.
        p. cm. — (The teen girl's gotta-have-it guide to)
    Includes index.
    ISBN 978-0-8230-1726-3 (alk. paper)
1. Teenage girls—Psychology. 2. Social skills in adolescence.
3. Interpersonal relations in adolescence. I. Frenette, Cynthia. II. Title.
    HQ798.B614 2007
    646.700835'2—dc22
                                            2007013980

Printed in China

First printing, 2007

1 2 3 4 5 6 7 8 9 / 15 14 13 12 11 10 09 08 07

To Leslie,
Lindsay, Lisa,
Maggie, and Liz—
my secrets to
Social Survival.

I love you guys.

nts

introduction

There's one thing you—yes, *you*, right here reading this book!—have in common with *every* other girl out there.

Whether you're usually the life of the party or you tend to be a wallflower or you often feel like an outcast, you've definitely found yourself in *some* kind of social situation that was no fun—and wished it would just hurry up and end already . . . haven't you?

Maybe it was that awkward family party where you were the only person under the age of 45. Maybe it was when your friends all got boyfriends while you were still single. Maybe you were the new girl at school, or had to give a speech in class, or were the only girl to not *really* need a bra yet.

See, from the class clown to the prom queen to the sports star to that quiet girl in your English class, *everyone* faces their share of uncomfortable moments. In fact, life can sometimes feel like it's *filled* with awkward situations—from big turning points like starting a new school to everyday drama like being separated from all of your friends for class.

That's where this book comes in. *The Teen Girl's Gotta-Have-It Guide to Social Survival* is your VIP pass for getting through the stressful, lonely, and just plain annoying scenarios *everyone* faces with style, confidence, and fun!

Good-Time Goal Sheet

The first way to start having more fun—no matter where you are or who you're with— is to think about your goals for the stressful situations in your life.

How do you *wish* certain situations would go if you had your way?

For example, if you're dreading an upcoming class trip because none of your friends are in your class and you're worried you'll have no one to sit with on the bus, your goal might be to connect with just *one* person before the trip so that you won't feel so alone. If you have a school speech coming up and you're terrified of talking in public, your goal may be to find a way to give your speech without freezing up. If your uncle's birthday party is coming up and you're bummed that you'll have no one to talk to, your goal may be to come up with a specific task to do at the party all day, so that you can avoid having to hang with the adult crowd.

Whatever scenarios you have coming up, write them all down here, along with a goal for each. Once you have a plan, you'll start to feel less helpless, and more in control.

SITUATION:

GOAL:

SITUATION:

GOAL:

SITUATION:

GOAL:

The Teen Girl's Gotta-Have-It Guide to Having More Fun, AKA: R.O.C.K. O.N.!

Whatever "type" of girl you consider yourself to be, there are six golden rules that will help you get through any drama:

RELATE When you remind yourself that *everyone* around you has been in your shoes at *some* time, you'll feel less alone.

be OPTIMISTIC Stay positive! A good attitude goes a long way.

say CHEESE Smile. When you smile, not only will you give out a friendly vibe that will attract people to you, but you'll literally start to *feel* better. Research has proven it!

KNOW the scene Be ready. Prepare. The more information you have about a situation you're going into, the less likely you'll be caught off guard and stressed out.

say "OHM" (as if you're doing yoga!) Unwind and stay calm. Learning how to stay relaxed will help you have more fun in any situation.

NETWORK Reach out to people around you. Buddying up with someone can make stressful situations more tolerable; so can having one trustworthy friend to vent to and turn to for advice.

the secret
confi

weapon: dence!

Confidence. Self-esteem. Assuredness.

They're all words that are easy for people like your parents or teachers to throw around. But, sometimes, it can feel *really* hard to find your inner confidence—especially on days when it seems like nothing's going your way.

But just a little confidence can go a long way in making stressful situations—and everyday scenarios—tons more fun. The tips in this chapter will help you build more confidence and find your inner strength when you need it most.

What's Your Secret Skill?

Everyone's good at *something*.

It may not be the "thing" that wins awards at school, but every single person has *something* they do well—and feel good doing. And the first step toward building more confidence is stepping back to appreciate what makes *you* special.

Maybe you're a star soccer player. Maybe you paint beautiful watercolors, or doodle hilarious cartoons. Maybe you're a whiz at crossword puzzles, or have a gentle way with animals, or always know how to cheer people up, or tell great stories, or are a good listener.

It's not bragging to admit to *yourself* what your strengths are. So use the next page to write down all of the things you're good at—no matter how big or small they may seem.

Once you've listed your special talents, come up with a fun and funky way to remind yourself every day of how amazing you are. Write a note on your mirror that says, "You have the best smile!" or make a T-shirt that says, "Animal lovers rule!" or underpants that say "I'm a good cook," or just add gold stars to your notebooks to remind you that *you are a star!*

My secret (and not-so-secret) skills:

Quick Fixes

Of course, even if you can appreciate a million and one wonderful things about yourself, you'll *still* have days when your self-esteem could use a little boost. On those days, try one of these quick fixes.

LEND A HELPING HAND. When you direct your energy to someone *else*, you'll shift your focus from you to them.

MAKE A TO-DO LIST. Make a list of tasks you know you'll be able to get done in one day—it's not cheating to include things like "call Grandma" or "fold laundry," and it will feel satisfying to cross stuff off when you're done.

WORK OUT. Exercise is good for your heart *and* your mind—getting your heart rate up releases feel-good hormones (called endorphins) into your system.

GIVE SOMEONE A COMPLIMENT. Giving someone sincere feedback on something they've done will brighten their day—and cheering someone *else* up can make you feel better in return.

LISTEN TO MUSIC. Listening to your favorite songs or finding new tunes on music websites is like therapy to the soul. Lyrics can touch your heart or help you get out a good cry, and energetic beats can pump you up.

FAKE IT. No good ever comes out of being phony—lying to yourself and to others will eventually catch up with you. But sometimes your mood and self-confidence *can* be a "mind-over-matter" situation. If you *tell* yourself you're no good, you'll start to *feel* like you're no good. But if you tell yourself "I can get through this!" or "I love a good challenge!" you'll be on the road to doing both.

HAVE A CUP OF TEA.
A mug of decaffeinated tea can help calm you down— you'll be forced to drink hot tea slowly, and slowing down can help you put doubts and worries back into perspective.

A FINAL NOTE

Building your confidence will help you get through whatever stressful situations come your way.

Take time each and every day to do the things that you love and that make you feel good about yourself.

relax!

Everyone reacts to stressful situations differently—and in their very own way.

Some people take on the role of class clown and boost their mood by making *other* people laugh. Some avoid the spotlight and just wait for time to pass. And some become so shy that they freeze up and start to panic.

However *you* handle not-so-fun situations, you'll be able to tolerate them better—and get past their downsides—if you learn how to relax. So read on for tips on how to unwind, stay calm, and have more fun.

How Should You Relax?

SNEAKERS

GOING HIKING

Your shoe rack is lined with:

MANUAL

STILETTOES

DIGITAL

AT A TRENDY RESTAURANT WITH A BIG GROUP

DISPOSABLE

Your ideal birthday party would be:

WITH CLOSE FRIENDS AT HOME

GET BUSY You enjoy being active, getting your hands dirty, and trying new things. The next time you're feeling stressed, take a power jog while listening to an upbeat playlist on your MP3 player.

PAMPER YOURSELF You're a high-style girl who appreciates luxury and elegance. So the next time you're feeling frazzled, spoil yourself. Go for a manicure, take a bubble-bath, or buy some juicy magazines and get lost in the celeb gossip and fashion pages!

BE ZEN You enjoy life's simple pleasures, and find comfort in natural beauty and people close to you. When life starts to get hectic, find calm in a long walk, a great book, or by writing in your journal.

Journal

Four Ways to Stay Calm

No matter what your personality type is, here are some quick tricks for relaxing in the heat of a stressful moment.

COUNT BACKWARDS. Close your eyes (if you feel funny, leave them open and just tune out everything around you) and slowly count backwards from ten to one. Forcing yourself to pause and shifting your focus away from the situation and onto the numbers will instantly calm you down.

TAKE DEEP BREATHS. Take a deep breath through your nose, feel your whole chest fill up with air, then breathe out through your mouth. Take five slow, deep breaths and see how you feel, then go back for another set of five breaths if you need to. Deep breathing will help you slow down, and it will also bring a fresh supply of oxygen into your body.

SQUEEZE-N-RELEASE. Clench both fists as tightly as you can. No, *tighter!* Now, go to the opposite extreme and stretch your hands and fingers out as far as they can go. Do it again: *squeeeeeeze* tightly, then release. Do it three more times. Feel better? That's because, without even realizing it, you've shifted the stress from your mind to your body in a simple, subtle way.

VISUALIZE. Close your eyes and picture the most peaceful place you can imagine. Is it a beach? A mountaintop? An open field? Picture what the sky looks like, what the sun feels like, what the air smells like. Focus for as long as you can on the details of your dream spot, so that it comes alive and you really feel like you could be there. Let it be a mini mental vacation. Then open your eyes, but know that you can return there—or anywhere else you can dream up—any time you need to.

Hooray for Hobbies!

It's impossible to avoid stress—school, homework, tests, friendships, boys, family, and everything else you deal with are a lot to handle. But the best way to keep stress to a _minimum_ is to make relaxing, comforting hobbies and activities a regular part of your life.

Whatever your interests may be, if you find a way to channel them into a hobby, you'll always have a relaxation technique you can turn to when the going gets tough. Here are some ideas for hobbies you can do alone or with a group, and within a range of budgets.

DRAWING: You don't have to be Leonardo da Vinci to enjoy drawing, and you don't need any kind of fancy supplies to get started. Pick up a pad of paper at your local drugstore, then experiment with pencils, pens, markers, or crayons to find out what you enjoy most. Doodle freely. Let your mind wander and see where it takes you.

CRAFTS: There are crafts out there for _everyone_. From scrapbooking to beading to collaging, knitting, sewing, or decorating your room, there are a million ways to have fun with glue, fabric, beads, and more. Head to your local fabric store and jump into a project you can make for yourself or as a gift for a friend or family member.

EXERCISING: School sports teams aren't the only ways to exercise. On your own, you can run, power-walk, or swim at a local pool. You can borrow DVDs from your library to try at-home workouts in yoga, aerobics, stretching, Pilates, Tai Chi, and more. And you can look online or in the phone book for classes in any sport that interests you—from horseback riding to karate to polo, badminton, Ping-Pong, and more. When you take the scoreboard and the goal of winning out of the picture, exercising becomes relaxing in a way that competitive team sports aren't. That's not to say that team sports aren't great—they are, and they're a fun way to meet new people, learn about working with others, and build your competitive drive. But, sometimes, they can get intense and stressful, too, which is why taking the time to exercise just for *you*—and no one else— can be more relaxing.

PUZZLES: Games like crosswords, Sudoku, word scrambles, jigsaw puzzles, and word-searches (there's one on page 91!) are a great way to stretch your mind without the pressure of competing against anyone else. Look in your local newspaper, photocopy puzzles at the library, or buy a book of puzzles at your local bookstore.

READING: There are books for everyone, from juicy novels to stirring romances to gory mysteries to inspiring biographies. Head to your favorite bookstore, or search your local library for books that pique your interest.

MUSIC: Listening to music and playing it can be equally relaxing. Always wished you could play the piano? Call your local music store and ask if they can put you in touch with a local student who can teach you. Want to build your music collection? Check out music websites, and sample everything from jazz to funk to classical to pop.

FOLLOWING THE NEWS: Reading the newspaper and checking out news websites will keep you in the know and give you something to follow every day. Plus, knowing current events will give you something to talk about with everyone—friends, adults, teachers, and guys.

PHOTOGRAPHY: You don't need a fancy camera to have fun taking pictures—sometimes a plain disposable camera can be more fun to work with since you won't worry about losing, scratching, or breaking it. Whatever camera you have, there are tons of things you can do with it. Take pictures of your friends, then surprise them with a collage. Document your pet's life. Surprise your parents with a family album. Or take pictures to document your home, neighborhood, school, and more.

COOKING: Whether you enjoy following recipes or experimenting, baking and cooking can be relaxing and gratifying. (And then there's the eating part . . . *yum!*) Ask the cook in your family if you can tag along when they go food shopping and help prepare a meal. Or check out recipes online or in a cookbook and whip up your own dishes. (And remember, cooking comes with some risks, so *always* ask your parents before you use their knives, oven, microwave, toaster, or any other kitchen appliances.)

GARDENING: Gardening is a simple way to unwind, and you can do it whether you have a big backyard, a small window box, or even some indoor space. Go to your local nursery and talk to a salesperson about what you have to work with to find out what kind of seeds or plants they'd recommend. Make sure to find out how much water, light, and care your plants will need. Then watch them bloom before your eyes!

JOURNALING: A journal can help you relax, unwind, and work out daily problems. Buy a plain notebook and fill it with your thoughts, doodles, poems, pictures, and lists. Keep it in a safe place or take it with you wherever you go. Decorate it. Put stickers on it. Fill it up and then start another one.

COLLECTING: Building a collection of something that interests you can be a lifelong hobby. Maybe you dream of traveling the world and want to start a collection of postcards. Maybe you love cooking and want to collect cookbooks from different decades. Maybe you love hats, or shoes, or comic books . . . the point is that *whatever* your passion is, there's a way to enjoy it as a collection. Start exploring thrift stores, street fairs, and flea markets. Look online or in your phone book for local auctions, or ask your parents if they'll take you to a meeting of collectors with similar interests.

A FINAL NOTE

Try to make relaxation a part of your life every day, even if it's just for a few minutes in the morning, before bed, or while brushing your teeth!

Learning to find inner calm—on a daily
basis and in the heat of stressful moments—
will help you handle obstacles and
have more fun!

about friends

Good friends are one of the most important things in life. With one by your side, any situation you face will be more fun and easier to handle.

Even when your friends aren't right at your side, just *knowing* in your heart that you have one best friend (or a whole group of friends) out there can give you confidence and help you get through tough times.

Making new friends can be challenging, and holding on to old friends as you grow and change can get sticky sometimes, too. But a good friend can change your life, which is why it's important to care for the friends you have, and reach out to the ones you'd like to make.

Is Your Best Friend the Right Fit for You?

Is your BFF meant for you, or is it time to move on?

1. When you tell your BFF that you got the part you wanted in the school play, she:
- a. Congratulates you.
- b. Tells you about the time *she* was in a play.
- c. Tells you that plays are weird.

2. When you and your BFF are around your crush, she:
- a. Showers you with compliments and laughs at all of your jokes.
- b. Flirts with your crush.
- c. Makes jokes about you in front of him.

3. When you get back to town after summer break and find out that your BFF met a crew of new people while you were away, she:
- a. Makes a plan for you all to hang out and get to know each other.
- b. Hangs out with you separately from her new friends.
- c. Stops calling you.

4. When older guys or girls are around, your BFF:
- a. Treats you the same as always.
- b. Puts on a cool front.
- c. Acts like you're barely there.

5. Who does most of the talking when you're on the phone with your BFF?
- a. It's pretty even.
- b. Your BFF.
- c. You.

SCORING

Mostly a's: Your BFF is supportive and nurturing and looking out for your best interests. Make sure you give her the same respect back—and don't be shy about telling her how important she is to you!

Mostly b's: Your BFF can be a bit self-absorbed. If you wish she'd devote more thought and attention to you, talk to her about it. Otherwise, remember that some friends fit different needs—maybe you have a friend who's self-centered but you keep her around because she makes you laugh. Just make sure you have at least one *other* friend who's there for *you* through thick and thin, too.

Mostly c's: It seems you and your BFF have grown apart—or don't have much in common anymore. It's time to seek out new friends who make you feel *good* about yourself. Use the tips on the next page to learn how to break the ice with new people and how to find the kind of quality friends you *deserve*.

Making New Friends

It was easy to make friends back in kindergarten. Your parents set up play-dates for you, your teachers put you in pairs at school, and all it really took was offering to share your snack or inviting someone to your birthday party.

But the older you get, the harder it can be to meet new people and make new friends. It's not like your school is constantly getting new students, and people have a way of sticking to the groups they form early on.

Still, there *are* ways to make new friends—no matter where you live or how big or small your school is. Here's how:

JOIN A SCHOOL CLUB. Try joining a club that your friends *aren't* in. It may feel awkward at first, but the activities at the club will force everyone to interact. And if you seek out a specific leadership role in your club—like being treasurer or secretary or president— you'll ensure that you'll have contact with new people and that you won't feel alone.

START A SCHOOL CLUB. Talk to your principal or guidance counselor about starting a club that doesn't already exist. Maybe you'd like to start a fashion design club, or a current events group, or a charity organization that works with children or the elderly. Whatever it is, make sure it's something you're passionate about—that way, you won't be turned off by the work it will take to launch it, and your genuine enthusiasm will naturally attract other people to join, too. (Bonus: Starting a club *always* looks great on a college application!)

VOLUNTEER. Volunteering outside of school—like at a children's hospital, nursing home, or animal shelter—will put you in touch with other student volunteers who don't go to your school. And, sometimes, having a friend who doesn't go to school with you every day makes that friend feel much more special—and opens your world to that friend's town, events, and friends.

GET A JOB. Working outside of school—with your parents' permission—will introduce you to people from other schools. Plus, it will teach you skills for future jobs and help you build a personal bank account.

THROW A PARTY. Throw a party with a twist—tell everyone they have to bring one person who no one else knows. That way, you'll have a mix of people you know plus new people to meet.

EXPLORE NEW PLACES. If you always go to the same movie theater or mall or diner, try making a change. The next time you need to study or do research, ask your parents to take you to the library in the next town. Go to a coffee shop you've never been to before. Explore your town beyond the same places you *always* go to, and you'll meet new people along the way.

JUST SAY HI. It's easy to settle into patterns and hang out with the same people all the time, or to assume that other people only want to hang out with *their* current friends. But when is the last time *you* said hi to someone in another social circle? Sometimes, all people need is a little push to open up. That girl you've been sitting next to in class *could* be your new best friend waiting to happen!

Conversation Starters

I love your new haircut!

It's not always easy to start chatting with a new person. But you don't have to let the cat get your tongue—instead, remember these tips, and you'll always have something to say.

ASK A QUESTION. Ask for the time, for directions, for a weather update—any question you ask (that actually relates in some way to the situation you're in) will automatically get the person you ask to talk to you.

SHARE A SINCERE COMPLIMENT. Giving someone false praise is phony—but if you can compliment someone on something *specific* and *true*, you'll make her feel more comfortable opening up to you. Tell someone that you liked her essay in class, or that she has cool earrings, or that you thought she did a great job at the game. You don't have to stalk someone, or go out of your way to find out information about her—just start opening your eyes and paying attention to the kinds of details that often go overlooked.

COMMENT ON POP CULTURE. If you start reading newspapers and magazines, you'll always know what's going on in the world (or even in the Hollywood gossip scene!) and have something timely to say. You can read many newspapers and some magazines online without having to pay for a subscription—try www.nytimes.com and www.usatoday.com to get started.

LEND A HAND. Hold the door. Share an umbrella. Offer to tutor someone in a subject that you're good at. When you reach out to help someone, you'll have something specific to bond over. That said, don't always put *other* people first. A true friendship involves *both* people working at it. Helping is a good way to make initial contact, but you shouldn't *always* be the one making all of the effort. (If you are, people will start to see you as a pushover or take advantage of you—and you'll end up resenting them, instead of connecting with them.)

How to Fight Fairly

Even the tightest friendships come with their share of drama. Whether you get frustrated with a friend or she gets mad at you, it can be stressful and awkward to deal with the bumpy patches. But there *are* ways to smooth them out. Here's how.

When *you* are mad at a friend:

ACT FAST. The longer you keep your feelings inside, the more likely they'll grow stronger. And that will only make things worse than they were in the first place!

TALK—DON'T "CHAT." Friendship drama is always worse online than in person or on the phone. So don't handle your fights with e-mail or instant messaging—speak up!

BE HONEST. Don't be phony. Tell your friend flat-out that you feel hurt by something she said/did/didn't do.

BE CALM. Don't yell or accuse your friend of something you think she did. Let your talk truly be a conversation in which you *both* speak—not a one-sided argument in which *you* do all the talking.

DON'T MAKE GENERAL STATEMENTS. Focus on the specific issue at hand—don't accuse your friend of "always" doing something or "never" doing something. Friendships aren't black-and-white, and making generalizations instead of being specific will only make you seem like you're exaggerating.

START AND END ON A SWEET NOTE. Tell your friend that you're upset about something, and that you want to talk to her about it because you genuinely care about her, and your friendship. When you're done talking, tell her again that you know these kinds of conversations can be awkward, but that it was worth it to you to risk some discomfort because her friendship is precious to you.

FORGIVE HER. If a friend apologizes, forgive her—don't rub the scenario in her face or hold a grudge. Agree that you'll both learn from the experience, and move on.

When a friend is mad at *you*:

HEAR HER OUT. Don't interrupt your friend while she's making her case. It will be tempting to jump in when you disagree, but hearing her out will keep you from being defensive. It will also force you to really *hear* what she's saying, instead of rushing to explain your side of things.

PAUSE. When she's done talking, really stop and *think* about what she said.

KNOW HOW TO SAY YOU'RE SORRY. It can be hard to say, "I'm sorry," even if you know you're wrong. Sometimes it's easier to rush to defend yourself because you feel guilty or embarrassed. But just saying those two words—"I'm sorry"—is sometimes all a friend needs. It shows that you care about her feelings, can put yourself in her shoes, and didn't mean to hurt her.

START TALKING. If an explanation is required, give it—simply. Don't talk in circles or come up with an excuse for what went on. Explain your intentions—it's possible that you hurt your friend without meaning to, or that you didn't realize your actions would affect her.

LEARN FROM YOUR MISTAKE. Promise you'll never intentionally make the same mistake again. Then commit to it!

KEEP IT BETWEEN THE TWO OF YOU. Don't go blabbing about what happened to your other friends. Write about it in your journal, or talk about it with someone who's not in your circle of friends—like a sibling or friend from another school. But gossip will only cause more problems later, and make your conversation seem less sincere.

DON'T BE A PUSHOVER. If you feel like you did nothing wrong, stand your ground. And if you feel like you have a friend who's *constantly* accusing you of doing something wrong, maybe it's time to take a break from that friend, and to give each other some time apart.

How to Celebrate a Friend: Friendship Day

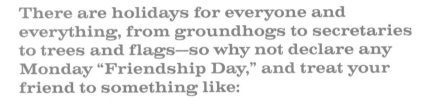

There are holidays for everyone and everything, from groundhogs to secretaries to trees and flags—so why not declare any Monday "Friendship Day," and treat your friend to something like:

FLOWERS: Buy her a sunflower or put together a bouquet of daisies. A floral arrangement doesn't have to be expensive to be special.

COOKIES: Whip up her favorite batch!

A CARD: Taking the time to handwrite a card can make someone's day.

MANICURES: Paint her nails for her, or treat her to a professional manicure.

A PHOTO GIFT: Make a collage, put your favorite picture in a frame, or go online for photo gift ideas from mousepads to mugs and more.

Now that you know the three "secrets" for social survival—feeling good about yourself, learning how to relax, and nurturing strong friendships—it's time to get down to business! The next few chapters will give you all the tips you need for surviving over 50 of the most common, stressful, and awkward situations!

And remember, there's never just one way to dress, act, hang out, or solve a stressful situation—for every situation that stumps you, think of the most natural, comfortable solution for *you*, then go for it!

A FINAL NOTE

You don't need a million friends to feel loved—the number isn't important. What is important is finding the *right* friends for you— and learning how to grow and strengthen your connection to them.

When you know in your heart that you have a bond with another person that can't be broken, you'll feel more confident when you're faced with situations on your own.

scenarios

School can bring with it tons of awkward situations–from having to give class presentations to trying to squeeze into your gym uniform to surviving classes that have none of your friends in them.

And there really is no way around going to school—it's a must for everyone and it takes up a whole lot of your time. So the best way to make it through any ol' school day is to seek out the activities you enjoy, reach out to teachers and counselors if you need some help (that's what they are there for), and study up on the tips in this chapter.

situation: You have an upcoming field trip and none of your friends are in your class, so you're worried about being alone on the bus or during lunch.

solution: You have a few options. You can bring a book or magazine to keep you company. Or you can talk to your teacher a few days before the trip to tell her about your worries and ask if there's some kind of task—like giving out the bag lunches, or making sure everyone has name tags, or even distributing and collecting some kind of worksheet or project related to the trip— that she can give you beforehand so you'll be guaranteed to be involved with the rest of the group. Also ask your teacher in advance if you can take photographs while you're on your trip— that way, when you get back you can share the experience with your friends who *weren't* there.

situation: You start a new school but feel like you can't break into the social scene.

solution: Moving is tough, but the best way to handle it is to throw yourself into it in a way that feels familiar. Seek out a team or club that you were on in your old school, and gradually you'll get to know the other members. It's also helpful to have a "tour guide" at a new school, so ask your teacher to pair you up with a student who shares your interests for the first few days. You may not instantly click or become best friends, but at least you'll have someone to turn to with questions about how things run in your new scene.

situation: You get your school schedule and none of your friends are in your classes.

solution: Treat your classes as a chance to meet new friends—and to meet new guys (why not ask the cutest one to be your study buddy?). And make sure that your differing schedules don't keep you and your friends from spending time together. Plan hangout sessions after school or on the weekends, or sign up for clubs or teams that you can bond over *after* class.

situation: You absolutely hate your outfit for a big event like a school graduation or awards ceremony.

solution: Personalize it! If your school makes you wear white to graduation, remember that you can wear something white in a style that suits you. If your dress for a school dance is too poofy, add a belt to it. If you feel like you're showing too much skin, throw a sweater, vest, or jacket on. When you feel more *comfortable,* you'll automatically start to feel more *confident* and, in turn, happier.

situation: You have to walk to school when all of your friends get rides.

solution: Come up with a way to put all that walking time to good use. If you like to take pictures, bring a camera along and photograph the streets through the different seasons to see how they change. If your parents are okay with it, take your MP3 player along and listen to your favorite music. Or just embrace the time alone to let your mind wander and calm down before and after your hectic school day.

situation: You show up at a school dance and someone else is wearing the same dress.

solution: It's annoying when someone shows up in a dress that you thought would be unique, but it's best just to make a joke out of it. Go up to whoever's wearing it—whether she's a friend or not—and just say, "Great dress!" with a wink or a high five. If you're truly looking for one-of-a-kind finds for future dances, avoid the major department stores and instead comb through the racks at vintage and thrift stores. Second-hand shops sell unique finds at inexpensive prices (that you can often bargain down even more)—and you can use the money you save to get your dress tailored to fit perfectly. You can also consider making your own dress—your local fabric store has basic patterns—or turning a regular dress into a one-of-a-kind statement by adding accents like buttons, rhinestones, ribbons, paint, or anything else.

situation: You feel self-conscious in your mandatory gym uniform.

solution: Talk to your gym teacher or the head of the phys ed department after class. Tell her you understand she can't make exceptions for one student without having to let *every* student bend the rules, but you were wondering if you could order a uniform that fits you better—and frees you to focus on gym class instead of on your outfit. Suggest wearing a shirt or leggings under or over your outfit, if that would make you more comfortable. And assure her that you're not being finicky about the *style* of the clothes—you're just being particular about the way they *fit* and how it's affecting your performance in class.

situation: You have to give a speech in class—and you're terrified of public speaking!

solution: Speaking in public is a very common fear. Here are some tips to help you master public speaking:

TALK ABOUT WHAT YOU KNOW. If you're passionate about your speech, you'll have more confidence. If you have to speak about a topic that seems completely unrelated to your life, *find* a way to make it relevant to your life, or to include personal examples—that will make the speech more interesting to you *and* to your audience.

DO A DRESS REHEARSAL. Ask your teacher if you can practice in the classroom or auditorium where you'll be giving your speech. If you'll be standing during your speech, practice standing. If you'll be sitting, sit during practice, too.

GET TO KNOW THE CROWD. If you don't have any friends in your class, start going out of your way in the weeks leading up to your speech to get to know more people.

KNOW THE SCENE. Check out the podium or microphone or any other equipment your teacher wants you to use in advance.

KEEP YOUR "SORRYS" TO YOURSELF. Don't apologize if you think you messed up—chances are, you're the only one who noticed!

FOR FURTHER HELP: Check out Toastmasters International—a worldwide organization that's devoted to helping people feel more comfortable speaking in public (and that inspired the tips here). To learn more, visit their website at toastmasters.org.

A FINAL NOTE

School can sometimes feel like one huge obstacle course—but you can make it more fun by trying to take advantage of everything your school has to offer.

And remember, if you're facing anything difficult at school, all you have to do is ask for help from your teachers, guidance counselors, or principal.

foibles
clashes

Friends are *supposed* to be the people you turn to for a *good* time, right?

Yet sometimes, friendship comes with its own share of frustration—especially when cliques are involved. But you can master the art of friendship and avoid getting caught in the tangled web of cliques if you surround yourself with the right people. Remember, friends should like you for who you are and not judge you for your opinions or dreams—and they should be people who you not only like, but *respect*, too.

Me
To: My BFF

situation: All of your friends are going to a movie that your parents won't let you see.

solution: Host a movie night at your house for other friends who aren't going to the movie. Rent DVDs, pop popcorn, and catch up on some long overdue bonding with friends from another school or your siblings or cousins—or anyone who won't be at the movie theater with the rest of your friends.

situation: A friend invites you to dinner at her house and you hate the food and/or have nothing to say to her family.

solution: Think of eating at a friend's house as an adventure, like trying a new restaurant or traveling to a new place. You don't have to eat *everything* on your plate, but try anything you're not allergic to. As for good parent conversations, even the most intimidating parents will respond to positive talk about their kids—so talk about something your friend (their daughter) did recently that will make them proud. Or ask them about a piece of art or furniture in their home that catches your eye.

situation: All of your friends are getting bras or sexy lingerie that you're not allowed to wear (or wouldn't fill out even if you could).

solution: It's a bummer to feel like all of your friends are growing up around you. But instead of letting it get you down, embrace it—do your best to "own" your late-bloomer status. Buy cute, funky bras as an answer to their sexy, lacy ones. Get funny boy-shorts and underpants with quirky sayings on them, instead of thongs (which are uncomfortable anyway!). And remember, everyone grows up at a different pace but, eventually, things have a way of evening out.

situation: Your friend starts fighting with her parents—in front of you—and you feel totally awkward.

solution: Excuse yourself as discreetly as possible—step into another room, check your voicemail on your cell phone, or read something nearby. After things cool down, tell your friend that you felt totally weird witnessing that—and ask her to please spare you next time. And if your friend or her parents turn to you for your opinion in the middle of their fight, politely say you'd rather stay out of it.

situation: Your parents expect you to take a visiting cousin or family friend along when you hang out with friends.

solution: It can be awkward to mix an "outsider" from another part of your life with your regular group of friends. You'll worry about making the new person feel comfortable and also about whether your friends will still have a good time. So plan a specific activity—like playing paintball or going bowling—instead of just hanging out. That way, everyone in the group will interact and no one will be left out. And before you go out, make sure you let your friends know that you're bringing someone new along. Tell them who the friend is, how you know her, what she's like, and about any sensitive topics they should avoid talking about in front of her. Then, do the same kind of "prep" with your family friend. Tell her a bit about the people she'll be meeting, and whether there are any specific topics to avoid!

situation: You're invited to a friend's religious or cultural celebration or event and don't know the customs or traditions.

solution: Not sure what to wear to a Quinceañera, or what kind of gift to bring to a Bat Mitzvah? Ask your host! Tell her that you're so excited for her big event and you're flattered to have been invited, and that you want to help her have the best time possible by being prepared. Ask her what the dress code is, what traditions you should be prepared for, and if there's anything specific you should bring or do or know. Then, do some research at your school library or online about your friend's religion, heritage, and customs so you'll feel prepared and confident when her big day arrives.

You're Invited
to My
Quinceañera

situation: You're out shopping and your friends are buying things you can't afford.

solution: Unfortunately, money is just one of those things that seems to create awkwardness even among the closest of friends! But even if you can't spend wads of cash, you can still have fun shopping with your friends by becoming the go-to expert on, say, shoes, or dresses, or jewelry. Read fashion magazines, go "window shopping" (look, but don't buy!), and offer your expertise. And remember, even if you don't have a lot of money to spend on clothes, you can have fun with fashion. When you go to a store, ask salespeople when their next big sale will be, then hit it early. Thrift shops and vintage stores often have great deals on one-of-a-kind finds. And if you're really lusting after something you can't afford, apply for a temporary part-time job to help you earn the cash. Babysit or rake leaves or offer to walk dogs in your neighborhood.

situation: You feel uncomfortable that your family is wealthier than your friends' families—or has flashier taste than your friends' families.

solution: If your family has a bigger house or takes more exotic vacations than your friends, you may feel ashamed or that people think you're "spoiled." But remember, *real* friends will judge you for your personality, not the size of your parents' bank account. To help you feel connected to your real friends, go out of your way to share common interests and experiences—join the same clubs, start a shared hobby, talk regularly, and be there for each other in good times and bad. True friendship can't be bought. The only real "currency" that matters with friends is loyalty, patience, and honesty.

situation: Your friends' families are wealthier than yours—and you feel like you can't keep up.

solution: It can be awkward, frustrating, and downright depressing to feel like your friends' families are in an entirely different league than yours when it comes to money. But if your friendships are genuine, the things that will keep you and your friends close will have nothing to do with money—they'll be about common interests, values, and humor. Still, it can get sticky when your friends can afford experiences you can't, or when they're talking about things you can't relate to because you haven't had the same opportunities. So go out of your way to make sure that you and your friends share experiences that have *nothing* to do with money—exercise together, join a club, or plan bonding sessions like movie nights and at-home spa sessions.

And don't be angry at yourself for wanting or envying things your friends have. It's normal—and doesn't make you a bad person. Just remember that "stuff" doesn't define who you are. If you really want more spending money, look into jobs after school or on weekends. Earning your own money will give you confidence—and you may even find that when you're the one earning the money (instead of getting it from your parents), you'll save it for the things that matter, instead of blowing it on things you don't really need.

Finally, don't judge your friends for having more money. Remember that it's their *parents'* money, not theirs, and that some day—if having a lot of money is important to you—you'll be able to go after a career that earns the kind of money you desire.

situation: You're traveling with a friend's family and they're all doing an activity you've never done before, like skiing or sailing.

solution: You may be nervous about seeming like a weirdo for not having the same skills they do, but speak up. Don't wait until you're in the middle of a lake to let your friend's parents know you've never water-skied before, or until you're at the top of a mountain before you tell them you've never snow-boarded in your life! And the next time a friend invites you on a family vacation, find out in advance what's on the agenda and if there are any special clothes, gadgets, or accessories you'll need to bring along.

situation: Someone starts gossiping about one of your friends behind her back and in front of you—and everyone else in the room starts to agree.

solution: You could say nothing or simply change the subject—but a *truly* loyal friend will make it clear that you stand by your friend, whether she's in the room or not. You don't have to make a big speech or get preachy, but say something like, "C'mon, guys—that's not fair," or, "Ouch, that's not nice." You can be lighthearted and brief, but as long as you say *something*, you'll be doing your friend a favor (and sparing yourself from feeling guilty later).

situation: You're better at something than your best friend—or she's better at something than you.

solution: If you're better, don't feel like you have to pretend to be bad at something or shrug off your achievements. But do go out of your way to do things with your friend that don't involve your special talent. So if you're a star athlete, do more than hang out with her at practice or talk about sports all the time. If you're a stronger student, don't constantly talk about school—focus on other common, equal ground. If she's better, look for ways to share other things that you're equally good at. Or start a new hobby *together*— like a music class or art workshop.

situation: You and your best friend are about to be apart for a long time.

Me

To: My BFF

solution: If you're going away, address and stamp envelopes to your friend before you leave. That way, you'll have no excuse for not keeping in touch, and you'll be able to mail her a letter or memento, which always makes people feel more special than regular ol' e-mail. If she's going away, throw her a little send-off party, for just the two of you or with other friends. When she's back, invite her over and fill her in on anything she may have missed, so she doesn't feel left out even though she was gone.

situation: A friend's loved one passes away—and you're not sure what to say or do to help.

In Deepest Sympathy

solution: The most important thing you can do when a friend is grieving is let her know you're there for her. Send her a card that says, "I'm so sorry for your loss. I'm thinking of you and your family and I'm here if you need to talk or if there's anything I can do." Call and ask if you can come over and keep her company, or if you can bring her anything from her locker while she's away from school. Ask a parent if you can attend the funeral, wake, or other religious ceremony. Even if you don't get a chance to talk to your friend at the ceremony, just seeing you there will let her know that there are people who are thinking of her.

situation: You want to hang out with your friends but you have tons of work and studying to do.

solution: Don't choose friends over work—it will only stress you out later. But what you can do is use the temptation of hanging with friends as motivation to get your work done quickly instead of procrastinating. Tell yourself that if you study for, say, two hours, you'll meet up with your friends for dessert after the dinner you have to miss. Or plan to work on a research project all day on Saturday in exchange for going to the movies Saturday night.

situation: You and your best friend are starting to drift and be closer to other friends.

solution: If you're drifting, make time to have a "friend date" with your original friend. While you're out, acknowledge that you might not be hanging out as much, but that you still love her no matter what. Or, if you think your two friends would hit it off, invite them both out for lunch or to go shopping. If she's drifting, don't just sit around resenting her. Call and tell your friend that you miss her and would love to hang out with just her, the next time she's free.

situation: Your friends are all talking about a party they are going to—but you weren't invited.

solution: First, make plans with a friend or family member you haven't seen in a while for the night of the event— that way you'll have something you're looking forward to doing. Second, let your friends know they don't have to feel awkward about it or keep secrets—instead, ask them about the party and ask to see pictures and hear stories afterwards. You'll avoid creating distance between you and your friends, and you'll also have your own special plans for the same night.

situation: You're at a party and the friend you came with ditches you for her crush.

solution: You've got two options—head home, or start hanging out with someone else at the party. The next time you go to a party with a friend, have a buddy plan in place. Agree that if either of you is going to head out with a guy (or anyone else), you'll let the other one know right away. You'll not only be keeping tabs on each other, but you'll also have advance notice so you can call home for a ride or buddy up with someone who isn't leaving.

situation: You want to go to a concert with friends but your parents will only let you go if they can come, too.

solution: As embarrassing as it may feel to have your parents come, realize that they make rules because they love you and want you to be happy and safe. That said, see if you can negotiate. Ask them to bring along one of *their* friends (or your other parent), so they're not just tagging along with you. Or ask if they'd let a different chaperone—like a cousin or cool babysitter—be your guide. On the night of the concert, have a specific meeting place so that if you get separated, neither of you panics and you can relax and enjoy the show.

situation: A friend is left out of a clique you're in.

solution: It's natural for friends to drift, but if you still feel close to the friend being left out, don't leave her in the dust. You don't have to include her in every activity, but don't stop reaching out to her because you're ashamed of her or don't think she'll fit in. (If you love her, true new friends will see her special side, too!)

situation: A clique is constantly teasing you.

solution: Ignore them. Giving a clique any kind of response will only encourage them to tease you even more. If they can't get a reaction from you, eventually they'll move on. Still, being teased can be hurtful, embarrassing, and painful—which is why you should talk about what's going on with your guidance counselor or a parent, who'll be able to help you work through your frustration and sadness. In the meantime, take comfort in this: The biggest bullies often act that way because they're insecure, or jealous of something you have that they don't. Don't let them talk you into giving up what's important to you or changing who you are. Before you know it, your uniqueness will take you places, and earn you respect and admiration—not taunting.

situation: You're in a clique that's giving you a bad rap.

solution: If you don't agree with how your friends are acting, talk to them about it. You don't have to lecture them, but talk it out and say, "You know, guys, I've been feeling really guilty/ uncomfortable/whatever about . . . " Then have a solution in mind—suggest you all apologize, or fix whatever went wrong— and commit yourself to changing your ways. If you really feel uncomfortable with the reputation your group has been getting and don't feel as close to the people in your clique as you used to, it's time to pull away and hang out with friends who make you feel proud.

situation: A clique has started to spread rumors about you.

What did I do?

solution: The best way to make a rumor die down is not to give anyone a reason to believe it. You don't owe an answer or defense to anyone who started a rumor about you. But if the rumor could get back to your parents or friends and cause misunderstanding, make sure to address it with them first. They'll be relieved to hear the truth from you—and they'll be there to listen to your frustration and cheer you up in spite of the false accusations coming your way.

situation: Your belong to two cliques, and they have started to clash.

solution: Be the peacemaker! It won't be easy, but convince your friends from both cliques—or just the ones who are clashing—to sit down and work things out. Tell them you know it may seem easier to keep fighting, but talking things out—or at least agreeing to disagree and moving on—will make everyone's life easier. Bringing them together will keep you from having to take sides—and keep them from wasting their energy on not getting along.

Beating Bully Drama: Learn to Speak Up—and Stand Up—for Yourself!

Sometimes, clique power can get out of control. If you feel like you're being bullied—physically, emotionally, online, or in person—it's time to speak to a trusted adult.

You may feel like a tattletale, but you'll be helping other girls (and guys!) just like you from being treated unfairly, too. And remember, getting help is a sign that you're able to stand up for yourself—and that you won't let people take advantage of you.

Seeking help can be scary—but it will be worth it in the long run. And even if some part of you feels like you brought on your own drama—or if you feel like you "deserve" the treatment you're getting because you were a bully in your past—know that you still owe it to yourself to put an end to the intimidation. (As for your own bullying past, now that you know how it feels, consider it a lesson learned—and promise yourself never to do it again!)

If you're being bullied at school or during school events, talk to a school dean, guidance counselor, or teacher. If you're being bullied outside of school grounds or time or even online or via texting, talk to a parent or other trusted adult. Take comfort in the fact that your teachers and school administrators have special training to deal with bullying in a way that will protect you and keep it from happening again. If the first adult you talk to doesn't offer much help, don't let that discourage you—reach out to another adult, because you *deserve* to be helped.

A FINAL NOTE

What's the perfect formula for having a good time with your friends?

Choose good friends who are good to you—and make sure to treat them just the same!

guy

drama

Boys _can_ be endlessly fascinating—they make dreary days brighter, add excitement to ho-hum scenarios, and keep you intrigued by what they say and do and how they act (or don't act!).

But sometimes dealing with them can be _so_ full of drama—like when your crush doesn't even notice you, or an ex spreads rumors about you, or when you and your best friend realize you both like the same guy! So what's the secret to handling those exhilarating-but-agonizing ups and downs in style? Why, a pinch of patience, a heaping cup o' confidence, and the tips in this chapter!

situation: You and your girlfriends are out with a group of guys—including your crush—and you feel like you're the only one who's *not* getting a chance to talk to him.

solution: The next time you go out with a big group, make sure to bring or wear something that will make you stand out—and give you something to talk about with anyone. That's not to say you should put on a show or beg for attention, but if you have some kind of "prop" on hand, you'll automatically have at least one obvious thing to talk about with your crush.

situation: You think you're going to have some time alone with your boyfriend, but your parents stick around or make the two of you babysit.

solution: Parents seem to have radar for when you want to be alone with your crush! If your flirty plans become family plans, make the most of it by letting your boyfriend see another side of you—show him how you can whip up grilled cheese sandwiches for your kid brother, challenge your family to Scrabble or Trivial Pursuit with him on your team, or head outside with your siblings and play basketball or draw with chalk on your driveway. Of course, don't surprise your boyfriend with the news that you two will have company. Let him know as soon as you can that your family will be involved, and offer him the chance to take a rain check for another day.

situation: All of your friends have boyfriends—but you don't.

solution: At some point, everyone goes through a phase like this, but it can be hard not to take it personally. The secret is to not always hang out with your friends in couples. It may feel like you're missing out, but if a scene is making you feel insecure, it's best to seek out something that makes you feel confident and good. Spend some time hanging out with another single friend, or focus on a hobby you enjoy, whether it's sewing, reading, or taking photos. Doing anything you enjoy will give you an instant boost!

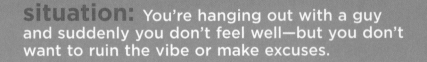

situation: You're hanging out with a guy and suddenly you don't feel well—but you don't want to ruin the vibe or make excuses.

solution: Be honest. Tell him, "I don't want you to take this personally, but I just started feeling sick in the last few minutes. I think I need to get home or something, but I really want to hang out again!"

situation: A guy you used to go out with starts spreading rumors about you—and you feel like everyone at school has heard them.

solution: If an ex starts telling people you have bad breath or are flat-chested or starts spreading *any* kind of tales about you, go out of your way to *ignore* the comments. Whether they're true or false, defending or explaining them will only give them power—ignoring them will help them fade away. Instead, focus your energy on something you love and are good at—before you know it, the only thing people will be saying about you is how great you did at your soccer game, or how gorgeous your new art project is, or how smart you are when it comes to math!

situation: You and a friend like the same guy.

solution: If he likes you, talk to your friend about it instead of waiting for her to find out from someone else. Tell her, "Listen, I know we were both kinda into [HIS NAME HERE], and even though he and I are sort of coupling off, I want you to know that you come first and that if you're really uncomfortable about it, I'll let things cool off. But I was hoping we could put any weirdness behind us and just move on." If he likes *her*, again, talk to her about it. Say, "I don't want things to be weird between us because of [HIS NAME HERE]. I know he's into you, and I'll admit that I'm a little jealous, but I'll get over it. And I'm happy for you!"

situation: You're leaving for camp/travel for the summer, and dreading being apart from your boyfriend.

solution:

It can be hard to leave a guy behind for the summer—you might worry that he'll meet someone else, or that things will change while you're away. So before you leave, talk about whether you really should stay together for the summer—or whether you should both be free to see other people while you're apart. (If you're the one leaving, it may be harder to offer this arrangement since the girls he'll be around all summer will be from your town. But you never know who *you* might meet, and not being tied down will let you find out.) Then agree to "check in" when you're back at the end of the summer, so you can figure out whether you want to get back together, or whether your time apart showed you that maybe you were better apart anyway.

Of course, if you're 100 percent gaga for each other, you don't have to *force* yourself to be apart. Instead, make a commitment to keep in touch as best as possible through e-mail, calls, or letters. And remember, sometimes absence *can* make the heart grow fonder—which means that you may come back and both be *more* into each other than ever!

situation: You find out from someone else that your ex is seeing someone new.

solution: Give in to your jealousy/sadness/frustration/ anger—for just a few days. Listen to sad songs, cry to your friends, write in your journal like crazy . . . then, do everything you can to have nothing to do with your ex, or the new girl in his life. Throw yourself into your friends, your family, your favorite hobbies. You may think you want to know every last detail about your ex's new relationship, but it will only drive you crazy and keep you from moving on.

situation: You go to a party and see for *yourself* that your ex is flirting with a new girl.

solution: Hearing about your ex being with someone new is bad enough—but to *see* him flirting with someone else (even if you were the one to dump him) stings like crazy. It can be torture to see him moving on—or to see a new girl getting attention from him (without her seeing his dark side!). But whatever you do, don't go over to them—find a friend, vent to her, then distract yourself by having the best time ever without your ex. The only way to get over an ex is to invest yourself into other things. If you do, before you know it you won't care who he's talking to or going out with because you'll be so caught up in your new life without him.

A FINAL NOTE

The key to handling guy drama is to keep it all in perspective. Think of guys like icing on your cake or sprinkles on your sundae—they can add something a little extra special, but even without them life is pretty sweet.

Whatever happens with guys, always remember the things that matter most to you—like your friends, family, and interests.

every

thing
else!

School, friends, and guys aren't the only things that can serve up social stress—pesky situations can crop up anywhere and at any time.

That's where this chapter comes in. It's meant to help you get through rough patches in every other part of your life, and to remind you that you're not alone—everyone has been up against a sticky, tricky, or icky situation at some point!

situation: You're at a party and don't know anyone besides the guest of honor, who's too busy to hang out with you anyway.

solution: Everyone's been to a party where they felt like an outsider—sometimes it even happens when you know tons of people there. The next time you get an invitation to a party where you won't know anyone, call the host and tell her you'd love to come, and were hoping she wouldn't mind taking a few seconds early in the party to introduce you to a few people. A few other tips to keep in mind:

1. You don't have to be the first one to arrive and the last one to leave. If it's an informal party and it won't insult the host, consider staying for just half of the party. Or make a plan with the person who's driving you that you'll call to let them know if you'd like to come home early or stay longer than planned.

2. Wear or bring something that's a conversation-starter. You may not want to boldly call attention to yourself if you don't know anyone else, but if you have a funky accessory or funny T-shirt, you can subtly call attention to yourself without having to say a word.

3. Wear your favorite outfit. More important than wearing something that gets attention is wearing something that makes you feel good. Find out in advance what the vibe of the party will be—jeans and tees, or dresses and heels?—then wear an outfit that makes you feel comfortable and confident.

4. Give yourself a task. If the party involves games, offer to be the scorekeeper; if it involves opening presents, offer to write down who gave what. You'll become an essential part of the group, and not someone who's left out and off to the side.

5. Let your body do the talking. You may not realize it, but your body language sends signals, loudly and clearly, to other people. If your arms are folded across your chest, people might think you're angry or not in the mood to talk. If your shoulders are hunched over, you may look moody or like you don't want to be bothered. But if you stand up straight, with a smile on your face and your hands at your sides or in your pockets, you'll naturally send a message that you're friendly and willing to meet new people.

6. When all else fails, stand near the food! You're bound to have something to talk about if you're near the table with the hot dogs or candy. If it's a sit-down meal, ask your host in advance to seat you near someone who's friendly and outgoing—that way, your host won't have to worry about "babysitting" you.

situation: You're away at camp and feeling homesick.

solution: Feeling homesick can literally make you sick—some people get stomachaches, feel nauseous, or can't eat at all. Homesickness is common and normal—but you *can* beat it. The secret is to distract yourself with an activity you love. The goal isn't to *forget* about home (you should actually bring a piece of home with you, like your favorite PJs or photos of your friends and your dog to comfort you!). But if you're focused on playing new sports or learning new skills and meeting new people, you'll have less room in your mind to think about home *all* of the time.

So instead of resisting the new activities at your camp, give yourself the chance to enjoy them—try new things, talk to new people, ask a counselor or group leader if there's some kind of camp project you can start or help out with. Also, find out before you go if you can set up a weekly phone call with your parents so that you have something to look forward to every week.

Finally, don't keep your feelings locked up. Write about them in a journal (it will help you pinpoint exactly what's making you homesick), and talk about your feelings with a counselor you trust and feel comfortable with. Above all, remember that being away from home won't last forever: You *will* be home before you know it, so make the most out of the experience and soak up all of the unique opportunities camp has to offer.

situation: You're stuck going on a summer family vacation, when you'd really rather be hanging out with your friends.

solution: Become the family photographer. Before you go, find the most durable, easiest-to-use camera within your price range. Then, throughout your trip, capture the places you go, the people you meet, and your family just goofing off. (Try taking candid shots, when no one realizes their photo is being taken, in addition to posed shots.)

Keep a notebook with you and write down a little description of each place you visit. When you get back from your trip, organize the photos and descriptions in a photo album or on a photo website. Taking on a fun job for the whole trip will give you something to focus on when you get bored, cranky, or just miss your friends and your room! (And remember, even if you don't have a lot of room in your luggage, you can take along a picture of your friends or your pets or your bedroom, or anything else you think you'll miss!)

situation: You're "the new girl" at camp and you don't know how to break into the group.

solution: It can be hard to feel comfortable in a group of people that got together long before you came along. The good news is that you're at the same camp, so you have at least *some* common ground, right? So instead of relying on generic conversation starters, talk or ask about things related to your new camp—and share a little bit about yourself, too. For example, ask someone what the food is like—then tell them you don't know how you're going to make it all summer without your mom's lasagna. Compliment a bunk-mate on her sleeping bag, and tell her about your search to find one in your favorite color. Or offer someone a few pages of your cute stationery to write home. And remember, you may be new to the scene, but you're not completely alone—*everyone* has been "the new girl" somewhere!

situation: You're getting driven home by the parents of the kids you babysit for—and you have nothing to say to them.

solution: Say something thoughtful and complimentary about the kids, like how nice it is that their older child is so helpful toward their younger one. Or ask a question about the kids' upcoming schedules, like whether they'll be playing little league or starting school soon. If all else fails, you can always turn to talk about your local sports team or the weather! Whatever you do, don't interrupt the parent when he or she is talking. When you're nervous, it can be tempting to chime in, but if you let *them* do the talking, you'll have less time to fill with your own chatter.

Why do you have pimples on your face?

situation: The kids you're babysitting make an unintentionally hurtful comment, like asking why you have pimples or saying that you smell funny.

solution: Kids don't mean to be cruel—often they just say exactly what's on their mind because they don't know enough about manners. If a kid says something hurtful, gently say, "That's not a nice thing to say—it hurts people's feelings and makes them sad." Then change the subject. Consider telling the parents when they come home, so they'll know what their kids are talking about if the topic comes up the next day.

situation: The kids you're babysitting aren't listening to any of your rules.

solution: Kids have a way of taking advantage of anyone other than their parents. It's just their way of testing their limits and seeing how far you'll let them push you around. So be fun— come prepared with games or projects you think they'll like—but be firm. *Tell* them when they need to eat, go to bed, and brush their teeth; don't *ask* them. Talk to the parents before you arrive about how flexible they are with things like bedtime. Sometimes, just reminding the kids that the rules are their parents' and not yours is all it takes to get them to cooperate.

situation: You have to go to a family event where no one else will be even close to your age.

Grandpa's Retirement Party

solution: Ask your parents if you can bring along a friend to keep you company. Or make a deal with your parents before the event that they won't leave you alone to get stuck in awkward conversations, and that one of them will hang out with you and introduce you to people you may not know.
If there will be a few younger kids at the event, ask your parents in advance whether you can be the official babysitter for the night; having a specific role will keep you from feeling bored or uncomfortable.

situation: You have to go to a hospital or nursing home to visit a relative, and you're feeling nervous.

solution: Talk to your parents about what, specifically, you're afraid of. Are you scared to see a loved one suffering? Are you scared to see other patients with bandages or hooked up to machines? If you tell your parents you're nervous, they'll be able to prepare you for what you might see. A good way to make yourself feel more comfortable about visiting a hospital is to prepare something special, like a card or floral arrangement or collage, to bring when you go. That way, you'll be able to focus on making a gift to cheer up your relative, and you'll think of your upcoming visit as a chance to give your gift, not as a day filled with the unknown. Another way to lessen your fear of hospitals or nursing homes is to start volunteering at one—you'll become more familiar with the environment, and you'll also help cheer up patients and visitors who could use your kind heart and cheer to get them through difficult times.

situation:
You're the youngest in your family and everywhere you go, you're compared to your older siblings.

solution: Even if you
look a lot like your siblings or have the same talents or interests that they do, go out of your way to start a hobby or learn a skill that's completely *different* from anything they've done. That doesn't mean you have to become a star athlete just because your sister was an artist, or you have to give up your love of music just because your older brother was a fantastic drummer at your age—but it will build your independence to try your hand at a new activity, and it will send the message that you're not simply a mini-clone of your siblings. Plus, trying a new sport, hobby, club, or activity will help you meet new people and open your family to new things, too.

situation: You're the oldest in your family, and your parents are stricter with you than they are with your younger siblings.

solution: It's common for parents to expect their oldest
child to take on a leadership role in the family, so see it as an *honor* that they have so much faith in you. But remind them that you're a kid, too, and that it can sometimes feel like an unfair amount of pressure to be expected to always be a perfect role model.

situation: You're the youngest in your family and always get hand-me-downs instead of new clothes.

solution: Whether you feel self-conscious about your stuff looking old or you're simply bummed that your parents won't splurge on new outfits for you, try to focus on the beauty of having older siblings. It means you have their successes and mistakes to guide you through life, and that your parents may give you more freedom since your older siblings paved the way for you. As for your hand-me-downs, you can personalize and accessorize them with your trusty glue-gun and some ribbons and buttons—then you'll have a new creation that's all your own.

A FINAL NOTE

No matter *what* you're up against, here is the key to surviving *any* socially sticky situation:

Make decisions that match your values and priorities—not someone else's—and that will make you proud when you look back on them.

the final exam

Now that you know the tricks to beating even the stickiest social situations, it's time to put everything you've learned into one handy cheat sheet. So fill out this "final exam," and keep it where you'll always be able to find it.

Star

1. **When I need a quick confidence boost, I'll try one of the following:**

   a. _____

   b. _____

   c. _____

2. **The best way for me to unwind is by doing things like:**

   a. _____

   b. _____

   c. _____

3. The friends who I can always count on to help me through tough times and laugh with me through fun times are:

   a. Name: _____

     Phone number: _____

     E-mail address: _____

   b. Name: _____

     Phone number: _____

     E-mail address: _____

   c. Name: _____

     Phone number: _____

     E-mail address: _____

Happy Friendship Day!

A FINAL NOTE

The secret to feeling comfortable in any social situation is feeling good about yourself.

The best way to feel comfortable is to find
out what calms you down, what you love
to do, and which friends make you feel good.
Then you'll be ready for anything!

extra credit!

Now that you're ready for even the most awkward social situations, it's time to start having fun right *now* with the exercises and activities in this chapter.

What is the worst situation you've ever been in?

How did you feel?

What did you say?

GET THE SCOOP!

Remember that "golden rule" on page 9 about taking comfort in the fact that everyone's been in not-so-fun situations? Well, now it's time to put your friends' and families' drama to good use—by finding out their tricks and tips for dealing with them.

On a separate piece of paper, "interview" your friends and everyone in your family about the most stressful, boring, or disappointing scenarios they've been up against—and how they dealt with them. Ask for their conversation starters, their favorite "props," and what they'd do differently if they could redo the scenarios they've put behind them.

You might pick up a few tricks and, at the very least, you'll learn new things about people you only *think* you know everything about!

WORD SEARCH

Can you find all of the words listed here? Look up, down, across, diagonal—and backwards!

BULLYING, CLIQUES, CLUB, CONFIDENCE, FRIENDS, GUYS, JOURNALING, MUSIC, PARTY, RELAXATION, SCHOOL DANCE, TEAM

```
S J E X J C E X B U L L L P A
C Q D F A L R O P P A R R C R
C U U R L L E E A N R U O C T
L L Q I F U O X R R U O J I T
O R F E E C N E D I F N O C Y
R E C N A D L O O H C S J C R
V L F D M G C O N F I D E L T
E A R S A T N S K O O L D I O
D X I E R T R I E S S V A Q L
X A E S P A R T Y B L C L U B
E T F Y J A M E S L A I I E L
L I R U K S S U M E L S L S O
A O I G G N I L A N R U O J O
Z N E E X J O U E R G M B D C
U Q R L A X X A T T U U Y I F
```

(answers on page 94)

Guilty Pleasures

Sometimes, the best way to get more clarity about a stressful situation is to escape from it for a little bit. So try one of these fun activities the next time you need an instant get-away or pick-me-up!

START WRITING THE STORY OF YOUR LIFE. Give yourself a new name and create a fictional tale about a character whose life is like yours—only different!

ORGANIZE YOUR CLOSET. It sounds boring, but giving yourself a simple task will give you a sense of accomplishment when you're done.

LEARN MAGIC. Go to your library for a book of magic tricks, then try them out for your family or the next time you're babysitting.

READ YOUR PARENTS' FAVORITE BOOKS. Ask your parents what their favorite books were when they were your age, then borrow them from the library and see how they compare to *your* favorite books.

MAKE A GREETING CARD FOR THE NEXT BIRTHDAY COMING UP. You can use all kinds of odds and ends from around the house to create one-of-a-kind stationery.

LEARN A NEW LANGUAGE. You may not be able to travel to another country, but you can start getting ready for your dream trip to Paris or Japan or any-where else in the world that intrigues you. Just borrow some instructional CDs from the library, and *voilà!*

CALL YOUR GRANDMA. It will brighten her day to hear from you, and she always seems to know how to make you feel special, doesn't she?

Time Capsule

Drama in my Life

My Goals

List
1. ~~~~~~
2. ~~~~~~
3. ~~~~~~

DO NOT OPEN FOR 10 YEARS!

Letter to Me

When it comes to social survival, time makes *everything* better. Over time, cliques will become less clique-y, you'll be more comfortable and confident, and you'll have mastered the art of having more fun wherever you go.

And because you—and the situations that stress you out—are going to change tons over the years, take time *now* to make a *Teen Girl's Gotta-Have-It* time capsule.

1. Find an old shoebox.

2. Inside, put a picture of you at the most fun party or event you've been to recently. Then, write a list of all the not-so-fun drama you've been up against lately, and the goals you have for making things more fun in the future. Add a copy of your list from page 8, and the names and contact info of your closest friends, with a note reminding yourself to look them up when you open the box some day.

3. Seal the box with heavy-duty tape and write "Private!" on it.

4. Ask a parent to hold it for ten years, or tuck it away in the bottom of your closet where you'll forget about it for the next decade.

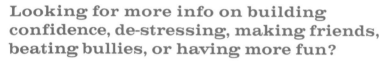

additional resources: the 411

Looking for more info on building confidence, de-stressing, making friends, beating bullies, or having more fun?

Try these resources. And remember, your school guidance counselor is trained to handle everything you're dealing with—so seek him or her out any time you need to talk to someone. And in case of emergency of any kind, call 911 *immediately*.

FOR SUPPORT, ADVICE, AND INFO ON YOUR GENERAL WELL-BEING:

The Center for Young Women's Health, Children's Hospital Boston
www.youngwomenshealth.org

Nemours Foundation's TeensHealth
www.kidshealth.org

FOR HELP WITH PUBLIC SPEAKING:

Toastmasters International
www.toastmasters.org

FOR HELP WITH BULLIES:

Stop Bullying Now
www.stopbullyingnow.hrsa.gov

FOR HELP WITH SUBSTANCE ABUSE, DEPRESSION, AND STRESS:

National Youth Violence Prevention Resource Center
www.safeyouth.org

index